Christmas TREES

Choose, Maintain, and Decorate the Perfect Tree

By Meg Crager

A TERN BOOK

Copyright © 1986 by Tern Enterprises, Inc.

ISBN 1-55584-008-6

Library of Congress Cataloguing in Publication Data
Crager, Meg, 1959–
    Christmas trees.
    "A Tern book."
    1. Christmas decorations.   2. Christmas trees.
I. Title.
TT900.C4C72   1986   745.594'1   86-5554

CHRISTMAS TREES:
Choose, Maintain, and Decorate the Perfect Tree
was prepared and produced by
Tern Enterprises, Inc.
Sagaponack Road
Bridgehampton, New York 11932

Editor: Karla Olson
Art Director: Mary Moriarty
Designer: Alison Lee
Photo Research: Susan M. Duane
Production Manager: Karen L. Greenberg

Typeset by Paragraphics
Color separations by Hong Kong Scanner Craft Company Ltd
Printed and bound in Hong Kong by Leefung-Asco Printers Ltd

Contents

When and Where to Buy Your Tree

I f you store your tree properly, you can buy it as early as three weeks before Christmas. Both cut and live trees are available from nurseries. Cut trees can also be purchased at Christmas tree stands that spring up at the beginning of December and from mail-order houses. Before you go to choose your tree, measure the area where you plan to put it, so you will be sure to get one that is the right size. Measure the height, being sure to include the stand. Determine the circumference of the area as well, to see how wide your tree can spread.

For an enjoyable excursion in the country, go to a Christmas tree farm and pick out your own tree. Trees you cut yourself usually cost less than those you buy at a Christmas tree stand or nursery. Remember, however, that it is illegal to cut your own tree from a private or public forest.

When you go to a tree farm, dress warmly, and wear boots, as you may have to tramp through mud and snow. Bring along a tape measure and a string or cord to tie the tree to your car. The tree farmer will supply you with a saw and instructions on how to properly cut down the tree, or he will cut it down for you.

Whether you cut it yourself or buy it from a stand, be certain that the tree you pick is the right height for your home; it is likely to be much larger than you expected when you get it home. If you make a mistake and buy a tree that is too tall, cut the excess height off the bottom to preserve the tree's shape. Decorate the mantel or window-sill with the excess branches.

Harvested or Living?

When choosing a Christmas tree, several factors must be considered. First of all, do you want a cut tree or a live tree that you can plant in the spring?

If you have a yard in which to plant it, you may want to invest in a live tree. As long as you have the proper soil and growing conditions, you can plant the tree in the spring and enjoy it for many years. However, a live Christmas tree requires more care than a cut one. A cut tree is lighter and easier to transport, for it does not have the weighty root ball of the live tree; a live tree can weigh as much as 150 pounds (seventy kilograms). In addition, a cut tree may be taken inside immediately, while a live tree must be kept in a cool though not cold place for a few days, so that it does not suffer from the sudden extreme change in temperature. Also, with a live tree, you must be sure to use the proper lights so as not to damage the branches.

When choosing a tree, you will want to look at its physical features: the length of the needles, the strength of the branches, and the ability of the cut tree to retain its needles. An ideal Christmas tree will have good needle retention, a full, symmetrical shape, and strong limbs to support ornaments and lights. It should have plenty of foliage with good healthy color, springy branches that regain their shape after being transported, and a pleasant aroma.

Choose a tree to suit your own taste. There are pines with long, pointed needles, and firs with short, blunt needles. There are vibrant blue-green spruces and elegant dark green pines. You may prefer a tall, slender tree with sparse, airy branches or a short, compact tree with lush, thick foliage.

Spotting a Fresh Tree

If you are selecting a cut tree, you want to be sure that it is fresh. There are two basic ways to test for freshness. First, bend one needle gently between your thumb and forefinger; the needle should be flexible. If it is brittle, the tree probably is not fresh. Second, lift the tree a bit off the ground by its trunk and drop it down again. A fresh tree will not shed its outside needles, although some of the inside needles will fall off. A tree is more likely to be fresh if it was grown in the area in which you buy it.

A live tree also is more likely to survive if it grows naturally in your region. The root ball should be securely bound, and the dirt around it tightly packed. Pick up the tree by the trunk (if it is not too heavy) and shake it gently. If the root ball wiggles, the roots have become loosened or detached, so pick another tree. Always carry a live tree by its root ball, not by its trunk.

A Catalog of Tree Types

The next thing you will want to consider is what kind of tree to buy. In North America, the most common types of Christmas trees are pines, spruces, and firs. The Scotch pine, Norway spruce, and Douglas fir are popular Christmas trees in Great Britain. Pine trees have relatively long needles that grow in clusters along the branches. The red pine (see page 20) has flexible, dark green needles. Native to New England, northern Pennsylvania, New York, West Virginia, and southeastern Canada, it will retain its needles for four to six weeks.

The soft blue-green needles of the white pine (see page 26) are about three inches (seven-and-a-half centimeters) long. It grows all around the northeastern United States and the Pacific coast of North America. However, the white pine does not travel well, so unless you live in these areas, choose another tree.

The Scotch pine (see page 23) has stiff blue-green needles that it will retain for four to six weeks. It grows in the northeastern United States, the eastern provinces of Canada, and on the Pacific coast, and it is indigenous to Great Britain. The Scotch pine (also known as the Scots pine) is a favorite Christmas tree in the Midwest in the

United States and in the British Isles. Some varieties of Scotch pine grow with crooked stems, which gives them an interesting shape. If you choose a Scotch pine with a crooked stem, make sure that it can balance on the floor or in a Christmas tree stand.

The umbrella pine (see page 27) is named for its soft, dark needles that grow along the twigs in whorls, like the ribs of an umbrella. The tree has a symmetrical profile, and its needles grow five to six inches (twelve-and-a-half to fifteen centimeters) long. The umbrella pine is native to the eastern half of the United States and the entire length of the Pacific coast of North America.

Spruces grow naturally in the classic conical shape of a Christmas tree. Various types of spruces can be found all over North America. The Norway spruce (see page 29) is cultivated as a Christmas tree in Great Britain. Spruces range in color from the dark

BLUE SPRUCE

RED PINE

green of the red spruce to the bright blue-green of the Colorado blue spruce (see page 19). Their needles, which grow singly along the branch, are short, stiff, and sharp-pointed. With their dense foliage and symmetrical shape, they make lovely Christmas trees. However, of the three types of trees—pine, spruce, and fir—spruces have the poorest needle retention.

Both the Norway and red spruces have a good Christmas tree shape and dark green needles. The red spruce is native to the Northeastern United States. The white spruce has short, blue-green needles that release a strong odor when they are crushed. There are several varieties of the Colorado blue spruce, all of which have a broad, conical shape and an attractive blue hue to their foliage.

Freshly cut fir trees have excellent needle retention and, for that reason, make especially good Christmas trees.

However, if shipped a long distance, the fir tree will lose its needles in a warm room. The needles of the fir have a pleasant fragrance and are blunt-ended, flat, and soft to the touch. The balsam fir is native to the northeastern portion of North America and has a good pyramidal shape with horizontal, rigid branches. The white fir grows in the western United States. It has bluish-green needles, dense foliage, and a good symmetrical shape.

Despite its name, the Douglas fir (see page 24) is not a true fir tree. Its fragrant, blue-green needles grow densely along the branch. Douglas firs are native to the Rocky Mountains from British Columbia to northern Mexico and are a favorite Christmas tree in the Pacific Northwest. They also are grown as Christmas trees in Great Britain.

When you buy a live tree, make sure that it is suited to the soil and climate where you live. Here are some general

SCOTCH PINE

DOUGLAS FIR

guidelines: Start by looking around at the evergreens in your neighborhood to see which types of trees do well. Then consult your local nursery about the particular type of tree that you want to grow. Most species need plenty of water and should be grown in an area that gets at least twenty-five inches (sixty-two centimeters) of rainfall a year. Young trees do better when planted in a sheltered spot, away from winds.

Pines need lots of sunlight and should be planted in well-drained soil that is not rich in nutrients. They will even grow in sandy soil, where they mature slowly and become compact and dense.

Spruces do best in full sunlight. Moist soil is ideal, but they can be grown in dry soil if watered frequently.

Firs need moist, well-drained, acidic soil and full sunlight. They do not do well in hot, dry climates and are badly affected by air pollution. For city conditions, the white is the hardiest of firs.

BALSAM

NORWAY SPRUCE

WHITE PINE

UMBRELLA PINE

How to Preserve and Care for Your Tree

There are a few things you can do to extend the lifetime of a cut tree. Until you are ready to decorate it, store it in a cool place away from wind, sun, and heat. Once you find a good storage place for it, trim the butt end at a diagonal, one inch above the original cut. This opens up the pores and helps the tree to absorb water. Then immediately plunge the stump into a bucket full of fresh warm water. You can keep the tree in a bucket of water until you are ready to move it inside. If you store the tree for more than a week, you may want to repeat the process of cutting and watering the stump just before you bring it into your house.

Whether you have a cut or live tree, it is important to keep the tree cool and moist to prevent it from drying out. Before you decorate it, mist the needles and branches with water, or give it a light, warm shower in the tub. Moisture helps a cut tree to retain its needles, keeps the boughs supple, and reduces the fire hazard. Sufficient water is necessary to keep a living tree alive. Put your tree up in a relatively cool spot, away from all heat sources.

A special mixture in the water may help to preserve a cut tree longer. Combine a gallon (four liters) of warm water with four tablespoons (sixty grams) of chelated iron (available at a household supply store), four tablespoons (sixty grams) of Karo syrup, and four tablespoons (sixty grams) of household bleach. The iron will help the tree to retain its color, the Karo syrup will give it nourishment, and the bleach will prevent the growth of fungi. Whether you use a special mixture or just fresh water, you must keep an eye on the water level. It should be checked every day and replenished when necessary.

When you purchase a live tree, make sure the root ball is intact and moist. The root ball will already be wrapped in burlap by the nursery or tree farm. The burlap keeps the soil around the root intact and holds in the moisture. The nursery may cover the root ball in plastic for easier transportation.

It is a good idea to water the root ball as soon as you get the tree home. Bring it into your garage or shed, or to a sheltered spot where you plan to keep it until you take it inside. If there is plastic over the burlap, remove it. You can water directly through the burlap. Water the tree gently but thoroughly with a garden hose or watering can. Before you rewrap it in plastic, let the root ball drain off excess water for at least a full day.

Never move the tree directly from freezing temperature to a heated room. Keep it in a cool, sheltered place for as long as possible. Before you bring it inside, you will want to cover the root ball in plastic to protect your floors from soil and water.

When Christmas is over, bring your live tree back out to the sheltered storage area. If you live in a cold climate where the ground is frozen, pack the root ball in straw and store it for the

winter, until the ground thaws. Occasionally feel the soil around the root ball to make sure it is slightly moist. If it is not, give it some water. If you live in a warmer climate where the ground is not frozen, plant the tree right away.

To plant the tree, dig a hole that is a bit wider and deeper than the root ball. Mix some peat moss in with the soil at the bottom of the hole, and pack it down with your feet. Carefully put the tree into the hole so that it is standing upright. Leave the burlap around the root ball as it will decay naturally. Pack the area around the tree with soil and peat moss. Cut the twine that holds the burlap around the root ball. Water the hole thoroughly. When the water is absorbed, replace the topsoil.

If you plant your tree in a windy area, it is a good idea to stake it to the ground for a year or two so that it can grow properly. And always make sure your tree gets plenty of water.

Make sure your tree is firmly balanced before you start to decorate it. A cut tree can be placed in a Christmas tree stand, available at nurseries and household supply stores. If your tree is over six feet (180 centimeters) tall, the stand should hold a gallon (three-and-a-half liters) of water.

Rest the plastic-covered root ball of a live tree right on the floor. Or put the root ball in a large bucket or round planter after you get it home and water it. During the few days that you store it in a sheltered place, the root ball will conform to the shape of the container.

Cover the stand of a cut tree or the root ball of a live tree with a store-bought felt Christmas tree skirt or a colorful piece of cloth.

If you have a very dense, tall, or top-heavy tree, secure it by tying a string to the top branches and attaching it to a nail in the wall or the hinge of a door or window.

Reducing the Fire Hazard

Take all precautions to make sure you have a safe tree. Start by untangling each string of lights to check for frayed cords, exposed wires, and broken sockets. Test each string of lights by plugging it in, and replace any burned-out bulbs before you decorate the tree.

All bulbs should face outward, to avoid direct contact with the needles. And always turn the tree lights off before you go out. It is preferable not to use lit candles on your tree; they are difficult to secure safely. If you do use them, make sure not to leave the room while they are lit and keep a fire extinguisher nearby. Also, paper and flammable ornaments should never touch the Christmas tree lights.

Decorating Ideas and Tips

Spend some time planning the design of your tree before you begin to decorate it. Have a good long look as it stands in your home in its natural form. Consider its height, width, and the density of its foliage. If it is a slender tree with long, thin branches and sparse foliage, use delicate lighting and a moderate number of ornaments. If it is a thick, dense tree with lots of foliage, it can handle larger, multi-colored lights and plenty of ornaments.

Also take into account the decor of the room and the amount of space around the tree. If you have antique period furniture, decorate the tree as it would have appeared during that time. A tree decorated with glass ornaments and silver balls looks nice with contemporary furnishings. If you have plenty of space around the tree, decorate it in a grand style. If the room is small, keep the lights and ornaments minimal.

Lighting is perhaps the most important part of Christmas tree decoration. It illuminates the tree itself as well as the decorations you put on. There is a wide variety of lights available, from tiny white ones to large multicolored lights with ornate clip-on bulbs. For the best effects with white or colored lights, look for clarity. Avoid the slightly yellow tone of many commercial lights.

There are two basic methods for stringing lights on the tree: the simple zigzag method and the more time-consuming in-and-out method. Using the first method, string the lights back and forth across the front of the tree on the outer ends of the boughs. Leave the side that faces the wall bare.

The second method takes more time but gives the tree greater depth. Carefully place lights in three or four places along each bough. Start at the top of the tree and place lights on the branches near the trunk first, then on the middle of the same bough, then on its outer ends. Go on to the next bough and do the same thing, until you have decorated the whole tree. This method requires many more lights than the zigzag method.

When you purchase lights, make sure they are approved for safety by your country's standards association: the Underwriters' Laboratories in the United States, the Canadian Standards Association in Canada, and the British Standards Institute in Great Britain. The association's insignia should appear somewhere on the package.

Two types of strings of lights are available: end-to-end lights, which have plugs on both ends, and those that have a plug on only one end. The end-to-end kind are easier to work with and are less likely to get tangled up. However, if you use this type of plug, make sure the connections are secure to avoid fire hazard. Never put more than six strings of lights on one end plug.

There are many different kinds of lights now on the market. In addition to the traditional teardrop and globe shapes, lights come in the shape of icicles, lanterns, glass balls, candles, and Santa Claus. Keep in mind that miniature blinking lights generate the least amount of heat and are least likely to singe the needles. This is especially important if you have a live tree.

Here are some general guidelines for how many lights, ropes of swag, and ornaments to use for a simply decorated tree.

	2–4' Tree (60–120 cm)	4–6' Tree (120–180 cm)	6–8' Tree (180–240 cm)
Number of Lights	50–100	150–200	200–400
Ropes of Swag	1–2	2–3	3–4
Ornaments	10–15	15–20	20–30

Motifs and Themes

The possibilities for decorating your tree are almost endless. From the very simplest to the most ornate, Christmas trees bring warmth and pleasure to your home. Here are some ideas:

With one box of varied ornaments and some careful planning, you can decorate your tree with a different motif every year. Look through the ornaments you already have to see how you might develop them into different themes.

For example, if you have Christmas balls in various colors, you can take out all the red balls and have an all-red tree with white lights. Or, if you have a few straw ornaments, you might want to collect a few more items to create a tree with a nature theme. Use pinecones and small seashells hung from from wire hooks. A simple tree is very striking; keep in mind that it is not necessary to use all your ornaments every year.

A monochromatic tree is elegantly evocative. Use white lights, clear glass balls, and white ribbons; or have an all-red tree with red balls, red tinsel, and red candle-shaped lights. You can decorate your tree in edible goodies—with cookies, foil-wrapped chocolates, popcorn strings, and candy canes. Create an angel tree hung with angel ornaments of all sizes, or a natural tree hung with gold-and silver-painted pinecones, polished seashells, and dried wildflowers and vines. You can even tie different color ribbons and bows around your tree. Greeting cards hung from gold thread make nice ornaments, too.

The seashore offers an abundance of material for a lovely and distinctive tree. Begin with an airy tree, such as a balsam fir, so the delicate seashells are not lost in the dense branches. Cover it with whatever the beach has to offer, or feature only one or two kinds of shells.

Sand dollars are very easy to convert to ornaments; run colored ribbons, primarily red, through their natural holes. Thread fine string through the center holes of fragile dried sea urchins.

With an electric drill, convert almost any of the harder shells, such as scallops. Run a long string through hundreds of (very fittingly named) jingle shells to create lovely oceanic swags. Draped deeply on the tree, they remind one of childish drawings of the waves.

Scatter red candles attached to scallop-edged foil bases around the branches of the tree. Top the tree with the ocean's own star, the starfish.

Decorate your tree using one color as the central theme. Create a gold tree with bursts of metallic ornaments and gold tassles, golden balls, and a swag of glass beads trimmed with gold leaves. A one-color theme can be used on any size tree, but if yours is very sparse, use fewer ornaments than shown here.

Start with simple yellow lights. The lights reflect off the gold ornaments, giving the tree a starry glow. Use plenty of lights so the gold balls are surrounded by a bright circle. Alternate tassles, white snowflakes, and bunches of clear glass beads, which will also reflect the lights. Hang little gold stars here and there around the branches.

Make gold designs on plain ornaments with sprinkle-filled glue, available at crafts stores in tubes. For an unusual effect, suspend metallic ornaments from the ceiling so they hang over the tree like bright stars.

Trim your tree with a menagerie of Origami paper animals for an exotic look. This decor is ideal for help from children. They will enjoy folding the bright-colored paper and seeing birds and fish and other creatures appear.

Make the paper animals from an Origami kit. Hang some from strands of gold thread, pushing the thread through the ornament with a sharp needle. Glue others to thin wooden dowels. Tie the dowels to the branches with string so they look like they are flying or swimming through the air.

Mix in other ornaments, but not anything too large or heavy that it would detract from the paper ones. Tie gold, green, and red ribbon on the branches. Wrap tiny boxes, and hang them from thin gold ribbon. Use the Origami ornaments as a decorative theme all around the house. Make creature placecards, and string a line of paper birds across the mantel.

A toyland tree trimmed with dolls is reminiscent of childhood pleasures. Choose a medium- to large-sized tree with strong branches and dense foliage. Place miniature white lights in a few spots along each branch to enhance the decorations.

Use several different methods for hanging the dolls. For smaller, lighter dolls, tack a few stitches with heavy duty thread into its back, then make a large loop. Tack in a few more stitches to secure the loop, and cut the thread. For larger, heavier dolls, insert an extra large safety pin vertically with the head of the pin going down into the back of the doll's clothing (if it's plastic), or of the doll itself (if it's cloth). Slip a wire hook through the "O" at the top of the pin.

Hang the dolls on the tree first, the lighter dolls at the top of the tree and the heavier ones on the bottom to keep the tree balanced. Fill in the spaces

with miniature rocking horses and other toys, lace-trimmed heart pillows, little wrapped boxes, and lace fans. Add a few red and silver Christmas balls. Use plenty of ornaments to create a plentiful toyland.

For a Christmas tree that sparkles with romantic charm, decorate with silk flowers, lacy ornaments, electric candle lights, porcelain dolls, and glass balls. For a new twist, swath it with strands of pearls. The tree will radiate with subtle white lights and splashes of pink, yellow, and red.

To frame these elaborate decorations, select a tree with sparse foliage such as a spruce or a fir. The abundance of decorations creates a playfully cluttered look, which would be swallowed up in the fullness and defined shape of a pine.

Making Your Own Decorations

If you have the time, it's always fun to make decorations at home, and young children will enjoy helping. Or make a few each year until you have enough for a completely homemade tree. What kinds of ornaments you make at home depends partly on what kind of tools you have. Scissors, needle, thread, and other basic household items are all you really need. Make strings of white or colored popcorn and cranberries and drape them around the tree in place of tinsel. Whole nuts in their shells make lovely ornaments. Paint them in gold or silver and glue a small hook onto the nutshell. Hang the nut directly from the hook, or thread a piece of string through the hook. Cut snowflakes and other lacy

Give glass balls a special theme by lifting up their metal caps and inserting brightly colored objects. Curl a paper flag around its wooden "pole," and let it unfurl inside the glass ball. Gently place dried flowers inside, one by one, or insert a bouquet of curled paper ribbon. A three inch (seven centimeter) length of sheet music or a colorful Christmas greeting looks nice inside the ball, too.

shapes out of heavy construction paper, or cover cardboard shapes with scraps of pretty paper or cloth. Paper chains also look nice encircling your tree.

Use cookie molds to cut plain cookie dough into animal and geometric shapes. Bake them and paint with a food-coloring glaze. Decorate the cookies with edible dots and sprinkles and hang them from the tree with ribbons.

With a jigsaw, you can cut all kinds of shapes out of wood. Paint the wood ornaments in bright colors and trim them with glued-on braiding, buttons, and ribbons. You can also make pretty ornaments with a sewing machine. Cut felt in the shape of stars, stockings, or little dolls, then sew the patterns into miniature pillows stuffed with cotton or fragrant potpourri.

Cut ginger cookies into attractive shapes with cookie molds. For dark cookies use dark brown sugar instead of light, and blackstrap molasses instead of regular molasses. Brush the baked cookies with a thin coat of confectioners' sugar mixed with milk, and decorate them with an icing that hardens.

Personalize a small stocking for each person in the family, then hang them all on the tree. Applique, needlepoint, or attach trim and ribbons to make each sock distinctive. Use a scrap from someone's favorite handmade dress for the body of the stocking, or steal an actual sock, as in the gray sport sock. All you will need for these delightful ornaments are some round-headed wooden clothespins, white wood, tempera paint, and odds and ends for trim. Cut limbs out of balsa wood for arms, and glue them on. Decorate the clothespins as Santa Claus, an angel, an elf, or any other creature you can think of.

With Origami, the Japanese paper craft, you can make colorful ornaments in all kinds of shapes for the tree or house. Origami sets with paper and instructions for folding are available at many toy and hobby shops.

Cut a scrap of pretty fabric into a five inch by twelve inch (twelve centimeter by thirty centimeter) rectangle. Prepare a twelve inch (thirty centimeter) strip of ribbon as a border. Saturate the rectangle and the border piece with liquid starch. Attach the border using the starch as glue. Fan-fold the rectangle seven to ten times into one slim strip. Weight it against a flat surface with a heavy book. When it is dry, gently open one end of the fan. Decorate the other end with ribbon and tassles. Hang the fan from the tree with gold thread.

Taking Down the Tree

Live trees should be kept indoors for as short a time as possible, as heat is bad for them. If the ground is frozen, store your live tree for the winter in a cool, sheltered place. Plant it as soon as the ground thaws. Cover it with plastic to protect it from extreme cold. Water it thoroughly and frequently, and stake it if you plant it in a windy place.

You will know it is time to take down your cut tree when the needles start to fall off. To prevent the tree from shedding needles all over your house, bundle it in a sheet or a large garbage bag and carry it outside as gently as possible. There are a few uses for a cut tree when the Christmas season is over. You can put it outside and use it as a birdfeeder. Hang pieces of birdseed-covered suet from the branches. Or chop the tree up for mulch or kindling. Another idea: The tree's branches may be cut off and used to protect delicate plants from the cold.

PICTURE CREDITS